Chapter 1

LOOK OVER THERE, AYA-SAN.
THAT'S THE JEWEL OF THE ORCHID CLASS: **SHIRAYURI-SAMA.**
?
SHIRAYURI-SAMA?
TMP...

Chapter 1 π4
Young Ladies DON'T PLAY FIGHTING Games
1
STORY & ART BY
Eri Ejima

ポト。
PLOP

....
O-
OH!

TH...
THANK YOU!!
TMP
SQUEEEE!

DID YOU SEE HER?!
THE WAY SHIRAYURI-SAMA HANDED BACK HER HANDKER-CHIEF...
WITHOUT A SINGLE WORD!!!
SIGH... はぁ
SHE'S SO COOL... ♡
HOW CAN SHE EXUDE SUCH GRACE AND POISE WITH A SIMPLE GESTURE ...?
OH, SHIRAYURI-SAMA!!
WOW. THEY SURE ATE THAT UP.
OF COURSE. STUDENTS RARELY ENTER KUROMI GIRLS' ACADEMY FROM OUTSIDE OF OUR LITTLE BUBBLE.
OF COURSE SHE'D BE THE TALK OF THE SCHOOL!
WE GRADUATED FROM JUNIOR HIGH TO HIGH SCHOOL, BUT THE FACES ARE ALL THE SAME...
AND SO IS OUR ENVIRONMENT.
JUST WHEN WE'RE ALL CRAVING SOMETHING NEW AND EXCITING, A BEAUTIFUL TRANSFER STUDENT APPEARS.
SO SHE'S AN OUTSIDER, JUST LIKE ME.
BUT UNLIKE ME...

※Translator's Note: "Shirayuri," or "White Lily," is not a common Japanese name, and would sound a little over-the-top to native ears.

EVERY-THING ABOUT HER TOOK MY BREATH AWAY!
SHE HAD MORE, OH, WHAT DO YOU CALL IT... POISE? AN AURA, MAYBE? EITHER WAY, SHE PUT THE OTHER PRIM AND PROPER LADIES OF KUROMI GIRLS' TO SHAME.
......
AYA-SAN?
I WISH I HAD HALF OF THAT.
UGH...
I'M SO JEALOUS.

I'D DO ANY-THING...
TO RADIATE THE AURA OF A "FINE YOUNG LADY," JUST LIKE HER!
KUROMI GIRLS' ACADEM

AT KUROMI GIRLS' ACADEMY...
AFTER THE END OF FOURTH PERIOD, THE STUDENTS HEAD BACK TO THEIR DORM CAFETERIA FOR LUNCH.
KUROMI GIRLS' ACADEMY
HIGH SCHOOL DORMITORY
GUH...
うげっ
AW, GREAT. IT'S ALREADY PACKED...
AYA-SAN!

WOULD YOU CARE TO JOIN US?
OH, WELL, IF YOU DON'T MIND...
A TABLE OF FIRST-YEAR CHRYSANTHE-MUMS JUST LIKE ME. LUCKY! ♪
NOW THEN!!
SHWIP!
......
I KNOW I THINK THIS EVERY TIME, BUT WHAT THE HECK?
EVERY MEAL IS AN INSTAGRAM HIT WAITING TO HAPPEN.
(NOT THAT I KNOW THE FIRST THING ABOUT INSTA-GRAM!)

AT FIRST, IT WAS GREAT! LIKE EATING EVERY MEAL AT A CAFÉ!♡ (NOT THAT I'VE EVER ACTUALLY EATEN AT A CAFÉ.)
IT WAS SO COOL! BEYOND COOL!! BUT NOW...
ぱく
NOMF
......
I'M TWO MONTHS INTO THE NEW SCHOOL YEAR...
AND THE NOVELTY OF EATING CAFÉ-GRADE FOOD DAY AFTER DAY IS DOING WEIRD THINGS TO MY HEAD...
It's delish, though!!
THIS CASSOULET TASTES JUST LIKE HOME, DOESN'T IT?
Tee hee!
OUR DEAR MAID WAS SO FOND OF MAKING THEM FOR US.
......

AYA-SAN, HAVE YOU GROWN USED TO SCHOOL LIFE HERE?
OH, ERR... YES, I HAVE! THANK YOU! (THE FOOD'S A WORK IN PROGRESS, THOUGH.)
OH? WHAT SORT OF FOOD DID YOU EAT AT HOME?
HUH ?!
DID SHE READ MY MIND?!
YOU SAID IT OUT LOUD, AYA-SAN.
......
HUH? WHAT?
WAIT, DO YOU SERI-OUSLY WANT TO KNOW?!
STAAARE
........!!!
THIS IS MY MOMENT!!
WHAT-EVER I ANSWER HERE WILL LIKELY BE OF CRITICAL IMPOR-TANCE!!
AT THAT INSTANT...
AYA BURNED A STUPIDLY HUGE AMOUNT OF BLOOD SUGAR TO ACCELERATE HER THINKING SPEED!!
T-MINUS: 1.4 SECONDS

IF I RESPOND WITH SOMETHING TOO PLEBIAN, I'LL DEFINITELY EXPOSE MYSELF TO PUBLIC RIDICULE!!
BUT SINCE THEY'RE PROPER YOUNG LADIES FROM KUROMI GIRLS' ACADEMY, AND THEY'RE CURIOUS ABOUT THE LIFE OF A STUDENT LIKE ME WHO TRANSFERRED IN FROM THE OUTSIDE...
US: 0.8
SECONDS
THERE'S NO POINT IN PRETENDING TO BE SOMETHING I'M NOT!!
SO WHAT DO I SAY?! I'M RUNNING OUT OF TIME!!
T-MINUS: 0.6
SECONDS
MMRGH...I KNOW!!! I'LL ANSWER WITH WHATEVER I HAVE THE STRONGEST CRAVING FOR AT THIS PRECISE MOMENT! AND THAT SOMETHING IS...!!
UMAKA-CHAN!!!
AND STUFF?!

PANT!
PANT!
WHEEZE!
HRNNGH!
HUNNGH!
WHY?!
WHEEZE!
GUUUUHH...!
YOU COULD HAVE PICKED ANY FOOD IN THE WORLD, AND YOU WENT WITH CHEAP-ASS RAMEN?! WHAT'S WRONG WITH YOU?!

UMAKA-CHAN?
YOU KNOW. INSTANT RAMEN?
It looks like this.
OH! I'VE NEVER HAD THAT BEFORE!
"YOU KNOW ABOUT SO MANY THINGS WE'VE BARELY EVEN HEARD OF, AYA-SAN."
"YES! AND NOT ONLY COURSEWORK-RELATED THINGS!"
SOMEHOW, A BUNCH OF PRIVILEGED YOUNG LADIES TRYING TO MAKE ME FEEL BETTER MADE IT HURT EVEN WORSE...
......
SIGH...
DEAR MOTHER...

YOU KNOW ALL ABOUT MY QUEST TO BE A PROPER YOUNG LADY.
THAT'S WHY I APPLIED FOR THE SCHOLARSHIP THAT GOT ME INTO KUROMI GIRLS' ACADEMY. WHICH IS GREAT AND ALL, BUT...
MASTERING THAT AESTHETIC IS GONNA BE A LOT HARDER THAN I EVER IMAGINED.
ぎし..
CREAK...
THE SPECIAL CLASSROOM ANNEX.
THIS PLACE IS A DEAD ZONE EVEN IN THE AFTERNOON.
TAK

パッ
TAP
パッ..
TAP...
カリ
CHAK
カリ
CHAK
パタンッ
KTAK
......
パタパタッ
TAK TAK
カリ..
CHAK..
パタッ
TAK
パ..
TAP...
カラ..
SLIDE...
パ..
TAP

"LOOK OVER THERE, AYA-SAN. THAT'S THE JEWEL OF THE ORCHID CLASS."
IT'S SHIRA-YURI-SAMA!
—...
AND SHE'S HOLDING A...!

CHAK CHAK
KLATTA
WHAP

BAM
BA-BAM
32
HUT!
FWUP
BISHHH
ZWAP
5 HIT
THWACK
WHAM
2 HIT
6 HIT
THWIP
THWIP
4 HIT
3 HIT

FWEEEEE
CHAK CHAK
I'LL BLOW YOUR BRAINS OUT!!
Chaotic Cancel
SHIIING

27
68
HIT
THOOM
CHAOS
BA-BAAAM
GYAAAAAH!
Fatality

You Win

HELL YEAH!!

......
......
HEH.
STOMP
HEH HEH...
HA HA HA!
......
AH HA HA HA HA!
HAH HAH!!

REALLY?! REALLY?! WAS THAT THAT THE BEST YOU CAN DO?!
YOU FRICK-IN' NOOB ?!
HOW'S IT FEEL TO GET YOUR ASS HANDED TO YOU TWO ROUNDS IN A ROW BY THE PLAYER YOU GRIEFED IN ROUND ONE?! HUH, LOSER?!
GO ON! TELL ME WHY YOU STOOD THERE TEABAGGING LIKE YOU'RE HOT STUFF EVEN THOUGH YOU'RE A MEME PLAYER AT BEST!
I'M JUST DYING TO KNOW!
......
THAT'S "114"...

!!!
GLARE
......
......

BLUUUUSH
......!!!
AH...
SLIDE...
I...
ERR...
Eep!
S-SORRY. I WASN'T TRYING TO BE NOSEY OR ANYTHING. I JUST--
CLASP!
UH...
U-UM, P-P...
P-PLEASE DON'T TELL THE TEACHERS!!

PLEASE! FOR THE LOVE OF GOD!!
I'M BEGGING YOU!!!
UH... D-DON'T WORRY...
I WON'T TELL ANYBODY...
カラカラカラ‥
SLIIIDE...
I SHOULD PROBABLY JUST...GO...
TUMP...

ATTENTION, ALL STUDENTS. QUIET STUDY TIME WILL BEGIN SHORTLY, AND LAST FOR THE NEXT THREE HOURS.
PLEASE RETURN TO YOUR ROOMS AS SOON AS POSSIBLE.
ONCE AGAIN...

......
HEY, BELATED QUESTION.
TUNK...
WHY DO WE HAVE TO GIVE UP OUR PHONES EVERY NIGHT, ANYWAY?
IT SEEMS KIND OF DUMB WHEN THEY LET US KEEP LAPTOPS.
CHAK
OH?
DIDN'T YOU KNOW, AYA-SAN? GAMES ARE PROHIBITED IN KUROMI'S DORMS.
......?
OHHH! SO IT'S THEIR WAY OF TELLING US NOT TO PLAY AROUND ON OUR PHONES WHEN WE SHOULD BE STUDYING?
EXACTLY.
BUT ALL GAMES ARE BANNED HERE, NOT ONLY SMART-PHONE GAMES. WHY, SOME STUDENTS EVEN GOT EXPELLED FOR BRINGING CONSOLES ONTO CAMPUS!
Not that you strike me as the gaming type.

407
深月 綾
咲坂 なつめ
TUMP
I SEE. SO GAMES ARE BANNED, HUH...?
YOU COULD THEORETI-CALLY GAME ON A LAPTOP IN YOUR ROOM...
BUT SINCE FIRST-YEARS HAVE TO ROOM TOGETHER, IT WOULD BE IMPOSSIBLE TO PLAY THEM IN SECRET.
THAT EXPLAINS WHY SHE WAS CORNERED INTO PLAYING MATCHES IN AN EMPTY CLASS-ROOM.
SNATCH
HMM...

Sign: "Mitsuki Aya" and "Sakisaka Natsume."

THE WHITE LILY, SHIRAYURI, ELEGANT QUEEN OF THE CAMPUS...
AND...
THE DARK LILY, KUROYURI, I GUESS...?
RE
YOU RICK-
BUT SHE'S TRYING TO HIDE HER DARK LILY PERSONA...
NO, THAT WASN'T A PERSONA. "SHIRAYURI-SAMA" IS THE MASK SHE WEARS TO HIDE HER TRUE SELF.
I'M WEARING A MASK OF MY OWN, SURE. BUT I CAN'T EVEN COME CLOSE TO RADIATING THE SAME ELEGANCE SHE DOES...
OH!
THAT'S IT! IT'S ALL IN HER FACE!!
AYA-SAN! ♪ COULD YOU COACH ME THROUGH OUR MATH HOMEWORK?
OH WELL.
IT'S NOT LIKE I'LL EVER INTERACT WITH HER AGAIN, ANYWAY.

GOOD DAY, LADIES!
GOOD DAY!!
LET US BEGIN OUR MORNING EXER-CISES!
LINE UP!!
YES!!
!!
ONE!!
TWO !!
THREE !!
FOUR!!

FIVE!!
SIX!!
SEVEN!!
EIGHT!!

WHISPER
ヒソ
LOOK. ARE YOU SEEING THIS?
WHISPER
ヒソ
...
YOU'RE RIGHT.
ヒソ
WHISPER
SHIRAYURI-SAMA USUALLY PUTS AS LITTLE EFFORT INTO HER EXERCISES AS POSSIBLE, BUT THIS TIME...
SHE'S CLEARLY FOCUSED ON SOMETHING TODAY.
WHO ON EARTH COULD SHE BE WATCHING?!
......
GOD, I'D KILL FOR A BOWL OF NATTO AND RICE...
FIRST YEAR CHRYSANTHEMUM CLASS

BIG NEWS, EVERYONE!
I COME BEARING A MESSAGE FROM OUR TEACHER.
WE WILL BE SHARING OUR NEXT GYM PERIOD WITH THE ORCHID CLASS!!!
SQUEEE!!
WHAT?! WHY ARE WE SQUEEING?!
SURELY YOU KNOW, AYA-SAN! ***SHIRAYURI-SAMA*** BELONGS TO THE ORCHID CLASS!
AND THAT'S ALL IT TAKES TO FREAK YOU GIRLS OUT?!
BLUSH
......

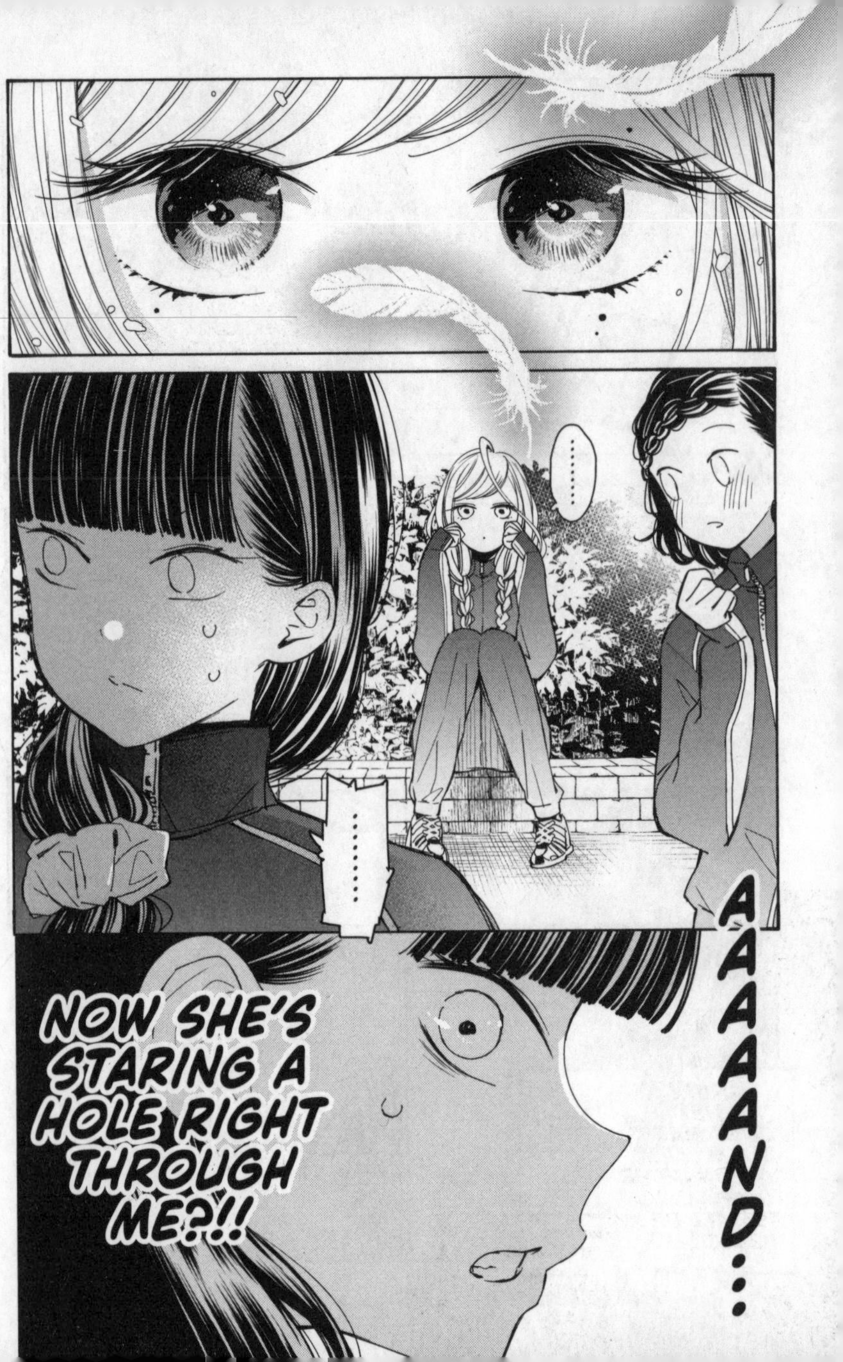
......
......
AAAAAAND...
NOW SHE'S STARING A HOLE RIGHT THROUGH ME?!!

WHY IS SHE LOOKING AT ME?!
IS SHE TRYING TO SEND ME A MESSAGE? LIKE, "HEY, BUDDY. YOU DIDN'T BLAB TO THE TEACHER ABOUT WHAT YOU SAW YESTERDAY, DID YOU?"
SHFF
I GUESS I COULD REASSURE HER THAT HER SECRET'S STILL SAFE WITH ME, BUT I DUNNO...
GIRLS?
WHO *IS* THAT PERSON SHIRAYURI-SAMA IS GAZING SO INTENTLY AT?
?!!
THAT'S MITSUKI AYA-SAN, ISN'T IT? FROM THE CHRYSANTHEMUM CLASS.
OH, THE SCHOLARSHIP STUDENT?
WHY WOULD SHIRAYURI-SAMA BE STARING AT *HER*?
PERHAPS THEY KNOW ONE ANOTHER?
THAT DOESN'T SEEM RIGHT. SHIRAYURI-SAMA'S ATTENTION SEEMS CLEARLY ONE-SIDED...
ONE-SIDED?!
ARGH! THEY JUST MADE IT A MILLION TIMES HARDER TO APPROACH HER ALL OF A SUDDEN!!
GULP...

SQUEAK
キュッ
THIS IS TOTALLY BIZARRE...
!!

KTAK.
And look who it is...
SHIRAYURI-SAMA'S PASSIONATE, SULTRY GAZE...!!
SHE'S BEEN STARING EVER SINCE THIS MORNING.
HOW SCAN-DAL-OUS...
I'M JEAL-OUS...
WHAT AN ENVIABLE DILEMMA!

キ BIIING...
コ BONNNG...
MATERIALS ROOM
OKAY, WHAT'S THE BIG IDEA?

SLIIIDE
......
LISTEN ...
KTAK
IF YOU THINK I'M GOING TO RAT YOU OUT TO ONE OF THE TEACHERS, YOU'VE GOT NOTHING TO WORRY ABOUT.
BUT, LIKE...
IN CASE YOU HADN'T NOTICED OR ANYTHING, PEOPLE ARE *TOTALLY* OBSESSED WITH YOU!!
AND WHEN YOU STARE AT ME NONSTOP ALL DAY, THAT PUTS ME ON EVERYONE'S RADAR, WHICH IS ALL KINDS OF AWKWARD!! NOT TO MENTION...

EVEN I--

WHAM
WHAM

DA- DOOOON...
......
......
......??
THROB!!
HUH?!
BA-DUMP BA-DUMP
WAIT, WAIT, WAIT. WHAT?!
......
EXCUSE ME? WHY ARE WE THROBBING, EXACTLY?!
HELLO, EARTH TO AYA'S HEART?! HOW IS THIS A "HEART-THROBBING" MOMENT?!

FLINCH
UH!
W-WAIT...
~~~......
......
PUCKER
ドキーッ!!
BA-DUMP!!
HUFF...
BA-DUMP!!
ドキーッ!!
......
MITSUKI AYA-SAN.
ULP!
ドキーッ!!
BA-DUMP!!
~~~

THESE...
ARE CALLUSES FROM HOLDING AN *ARCADE STICK*, AREN'T THEY?

BLUSH
わぁ
HUH?
AND, UM...
YOU WHISPERED SOMETHING FROM THE DOORWAY YESTERDAY.
An arcade-style controller.
YOU SAID π4.
RIGHT? I HEARD YOU.
.........!!
※π4: an abbreviation of the fighting game *Iron Senpai 4*.
IT...IT MUST HAVE SLIPPED OUT...

THERE'S NO WAY YOU COULD HAVE SEEN MY MONITOR FROM WHERE YOU WERE STANDING...
RIGHT?
YOU COULDN'T HAVE. SO...
THE FACT YOU COULD TELL I WAS PLAYING IRON SENPAI...
SPECIFICALLY, IRON SENPAI 4, JUST FROM THE SOUND...
(Speed talking)
WHAT THAT MEANS IS...
B-BASICALLY, YOU...!!
Y-Y-Y-YOU'RE A FIGHTING GAME--NRGH ...!!
GUHF!

YUH, YUH...
YOU...
PLIP
WHEEZE!
YOU P...
HAHEE!
P-PLAY...
FUH...!
FIGHT-ING...!!
PANT!
Y-Y-YOU T-T-TOTALLY PLAY FIGHTING GAMES, DON'T YOU?!
SPLAP
SPLORT

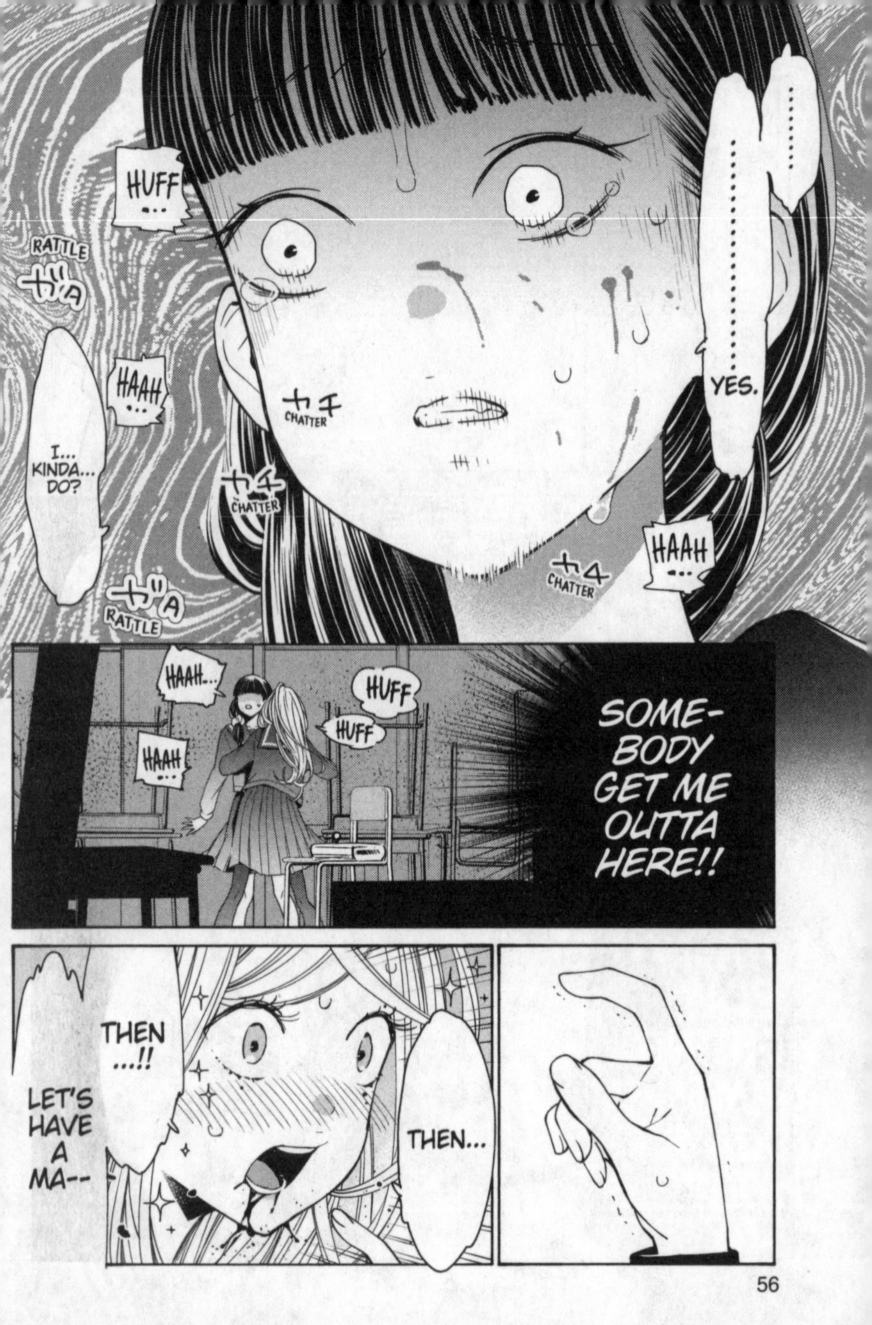

YES.
HAAH...
カチ CHATTER
HUFF...
カチ CHATTER
カチ CHATTER
HAAH...
ガタ RATTLE
I... KINDA... DO?
ガタ RATTLE
SOME-BODY GET ME OUTTA HERE!!
HUFF
HUFF
HAAH...
HAAH...
THEN...
THEN ...!!
LET'S HAVE A MA--

NO. SORRY.
I...
QUIT FIGHTING GAMES.
?!
......
YOU...
QUIT ...?
WHY...? WHY WOULD YOU DO THAT?

DOES A PROPER YOUNG LADY KNOW HOW TO EXECUTE A PADC-METSU?
......
......?
.........???
"WHAT'S A PADC," YOU ASK?!
YOU DO AN EX PARRY & ATTACK STARTING WITH THE FIRST HIT OF THE RISING FIST AND CANCEL IMMEDIATELY INTO A FORWARD DASH!
Rising Fist
Forward-dash to parry cancel
THEN YOU JUGGLE YOUR OPPONENT WITH A METSU HADOU SATSU!!
METSU
10HIT COMBO
THIS IS AN ADVANCED PIECE OF TECH FROM π3U, THE PREDECESSOR TO π4!
Well, yeah, I know that...

※π3U: short for *Iron Senpai 3: Ultra Dash*.

DO PROPER YOUNG LADIES DO MEDIUM KICK HIT CONFIRMS?
WHAT ABOUT COMPLEX COMMAND GRABS?
CAN THEY CHAIN AN INFINITE THROW LOOP ON WAKE-UP WITH FRAME-PERFECT PRECISION?
NO!!!
THEY ABSO-LUTELY CAN'T!!
FIGHTING GAMES ARE A BARBARIC PASTIME AS FAR AS YOU CAN POSSIBLY GET FROM THE PRO-PRIETY OF A YOUNG LADY!!
...
I CHOSE TO LEAVE THAT ALL BEHIND...
SO I COULD BE A WELL-MANNERED YOUNG LADY.
SO, SORRY, BUT I'M NOT PLAYING YOUR GAME.

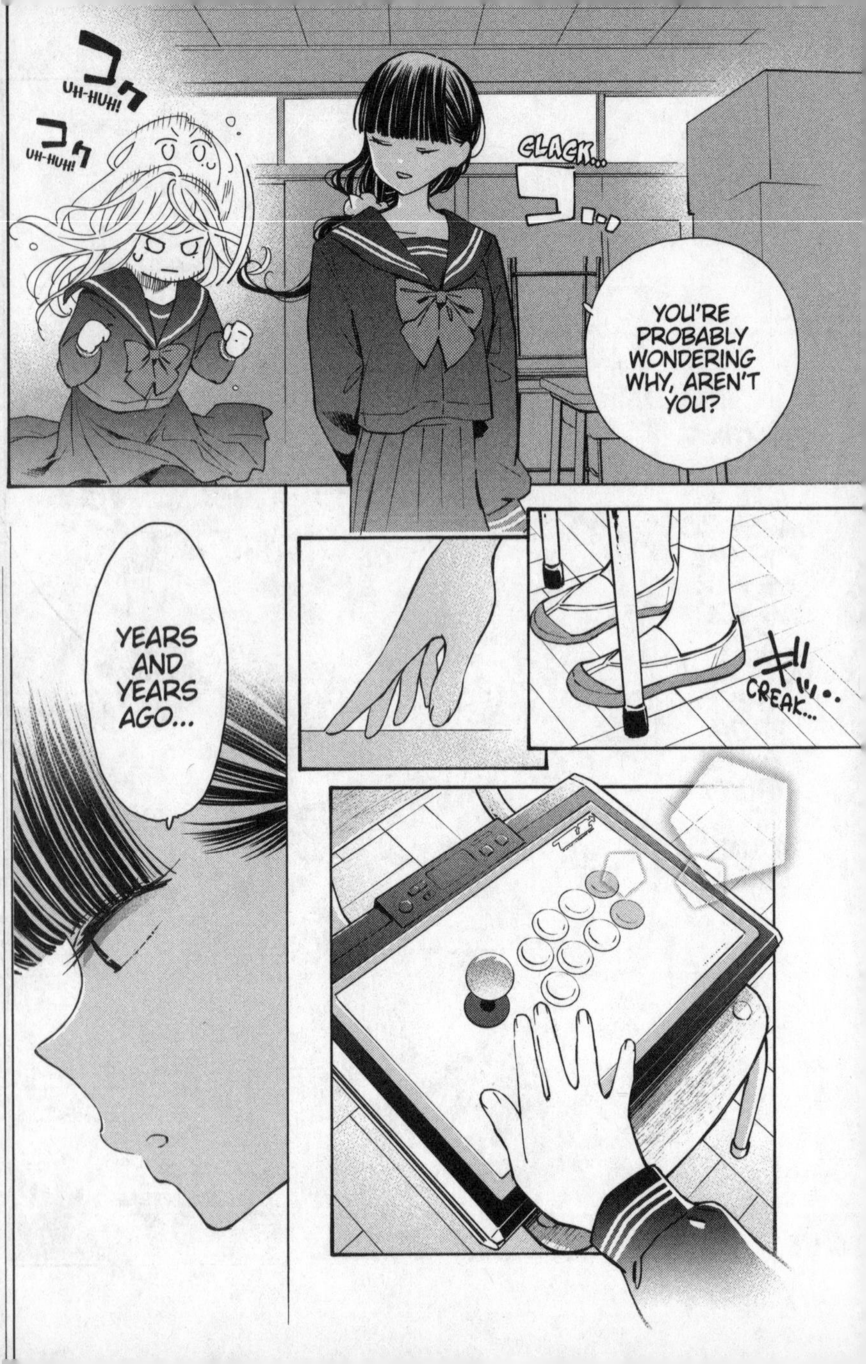
CLACK...
YOU'RE PROBABLY WONDERING WHY, AREN'T YOU?
UH-HUH!
UH-HUH!
CREAK...
YEARS AND YEARS AGO...

MY WORLD USED TO SHINE LIKE DIAMONDS.
BECAUSE I HAD SOMETHING I LOVED.
"HEY, MITSUKI!!"

WE'RE HAVING A π2 TOURNAMENT AT TAKEDA'S PLACE!!
Double-elimina-tion-style!!
YOU'RE PLAYIN' WITH US WHETHER YOU WANT TO OR NOT!!
WHAP

※Double elimination: Once a player loses a match, they are moved into the losers' bracket. They are only eliminated from the tournament after losing a match there.

A.K.A., π2.
Iron Senpai 2...
Iron Senpai 2
At the time, it was the precursor to a massive gaming boom that took the world by storm.
AW, SHUT UP!
I'M TOTALLY GONNA MAKE YOU CRY THIS TIME!!
AWW, DO YOU BOYS NEED ME TO TAKE YOU TO SCHOOL AGAIN?
Fine by me!
HEH HEH HEH!

Barely any of the girls my age gave it a second look...
ZE!!
GUH!
HI-YAH!
but I joined the boys and played my heart out.
My heart would race...
swept up in the thrill of battle.
I wanted to bask in that feeling of excitement, so I obsessively worked on improving my game.

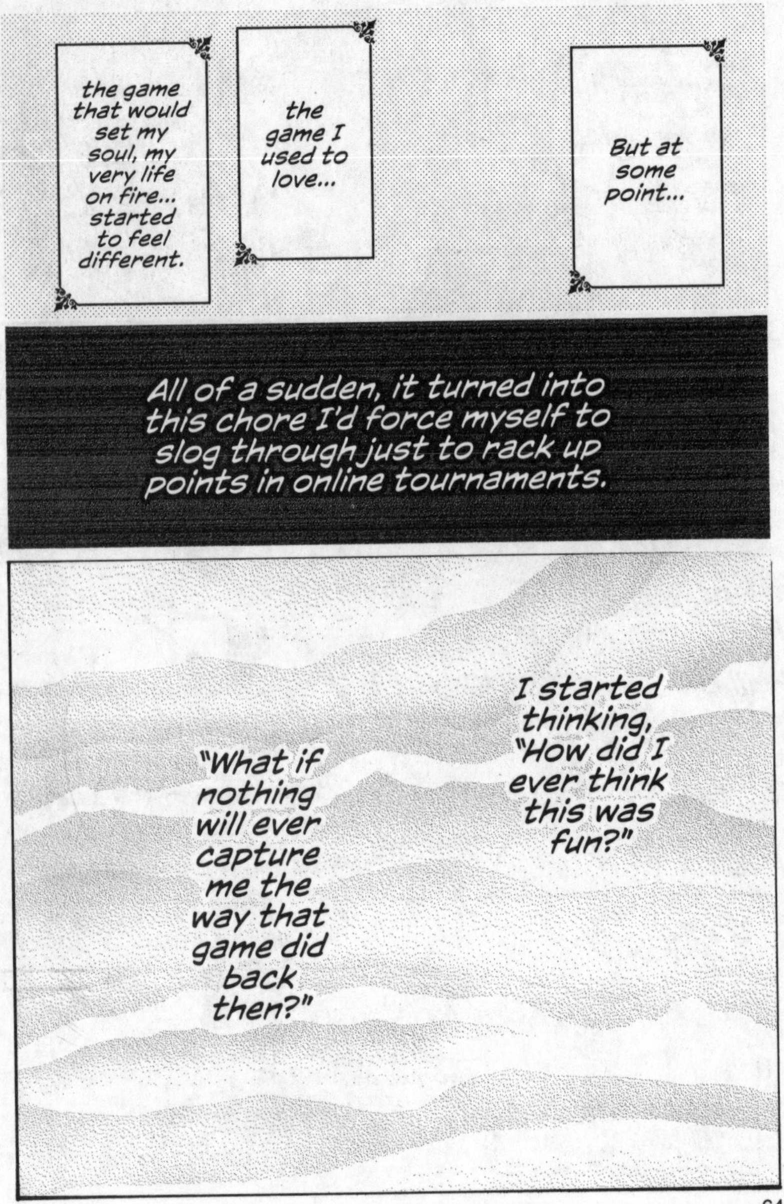

But at some point...
the game I used to love...
the game that would set my soul, my very life on fire... started to feel different.
All of a sudden, it turned into this chore I'd force myself to slog through just to rack up points in online tournaments.
I started thinking, "How did I ever think this was fun?"
"What if nothing will ever capture me the way that game did back then?"

AND THAT TERRIFIED ME.
TMP...
I FIGURED I COULD TRY TURNING MY WORLD UPSIDE DOWN, JUST TO SEE WHAT WOULD HAPPEN...
SO I APPLIED TO KUROMI.
SOMETHING TOLD ME I WOULDN'T KNOW WHAT FUN WAS UNLESS I REALLY WENT ALL OUT, SO...
I DECIDED TO MASTER THE ART OF BEING A PROPER YOUNG LADY.
AND THAT'S... ALL THERE IS TO IT.
......
WOW, UM...

I HAVE ABSOLUTELY ZERO IDEA WHAT YOU'RE TALKING ABOUT.
?!!
JUST PLAY A GAME WITH ME, OKAY?

WHY ...?
......
......
......
WHY WOULD YOU EVER ASK *WHY*?
"WHY"?

I ASKED BECAUSE I WANT TO PLAY AGAINST YOU!!
HOW CAN IT BE MORE OBVIOUS THAN THAT?!!
SPARE ME YOUR *DIAMONDS!*
I DON'T CARE ABOUT YOUR *BURNING SOUL!!*

I DID YOU A FAVOR AND SAT THROUGH YOUR CRINGEY, POINTLESS MONOLOGUE! THE LEAST YOU COULD DO IS PAY ME BACK WITH A GAME!!
SHUT UP AND FIGHT ME!!

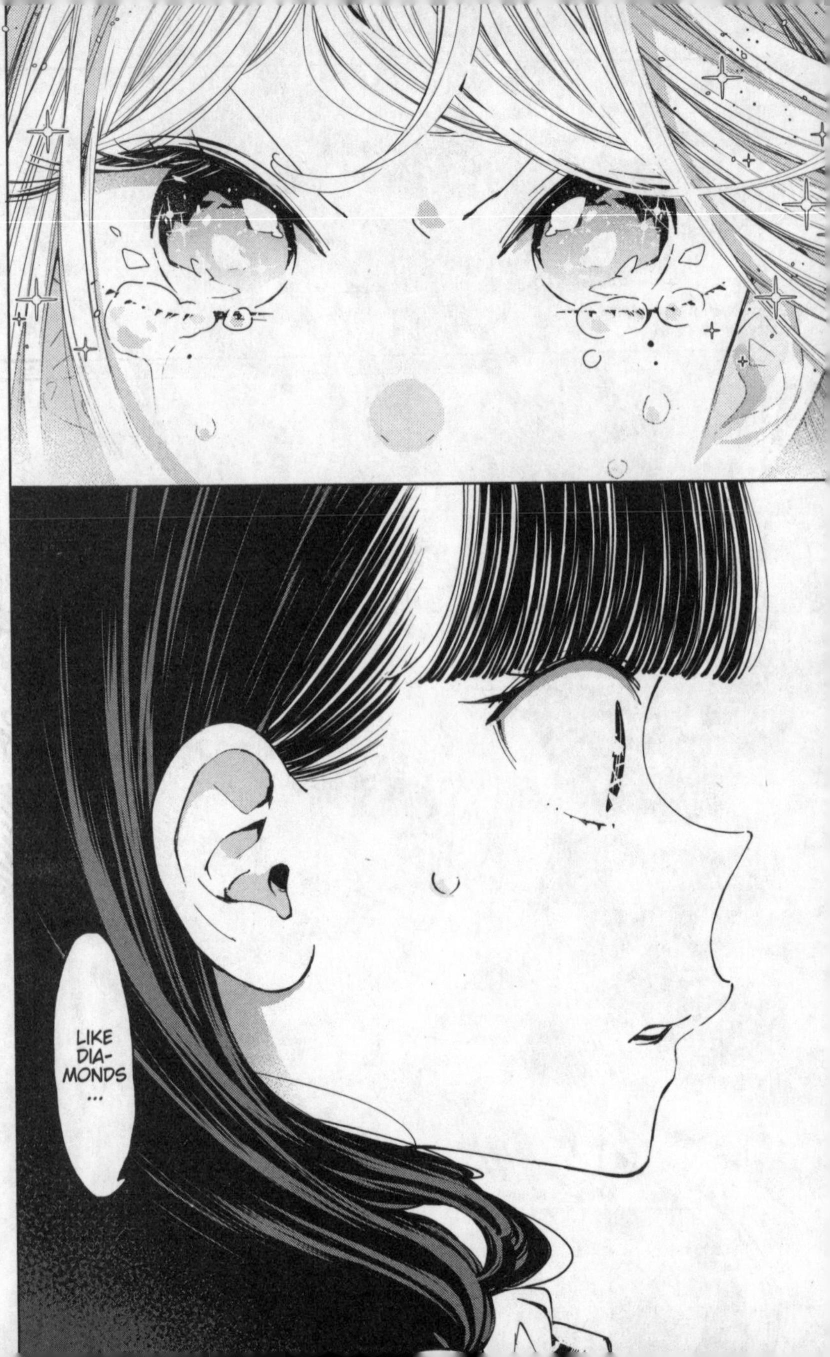
LIKE DIA- MONDS ...

I KNEW IT WAS BREAKING THE RULES.
THERE WASN'T A SHRED OF LOGIC BEHIND MY DECISION.
DON'T GET ME WRONG, IT WASN'T AS THOUGH SHE SWAYED ME WITH HER PASSION.
I DIDN'T FEEL SOME MYSTERIOUS FORCE TELLING ME TO DO IT, EITHER.
I JUST...
PA-SHIIING
CHOOSE YOUR CHARAC-TER!
KCHAK
KCHAK
I THOUGHT THAT MAYBE IF I AGREED TO HER GAME, THEN MAYBE MY EYES WOULD SHINE LIKE HERS DID.

DA-DUNNNN...
GET READY FOR THE NEXT BATTLE!
I KNOW IT SOUNDS STUPID. BUT THAT'S WHAT I THOUGHT.
Chapter 1 /END

Chapter 2 I'll Never Play Fighting Games Again

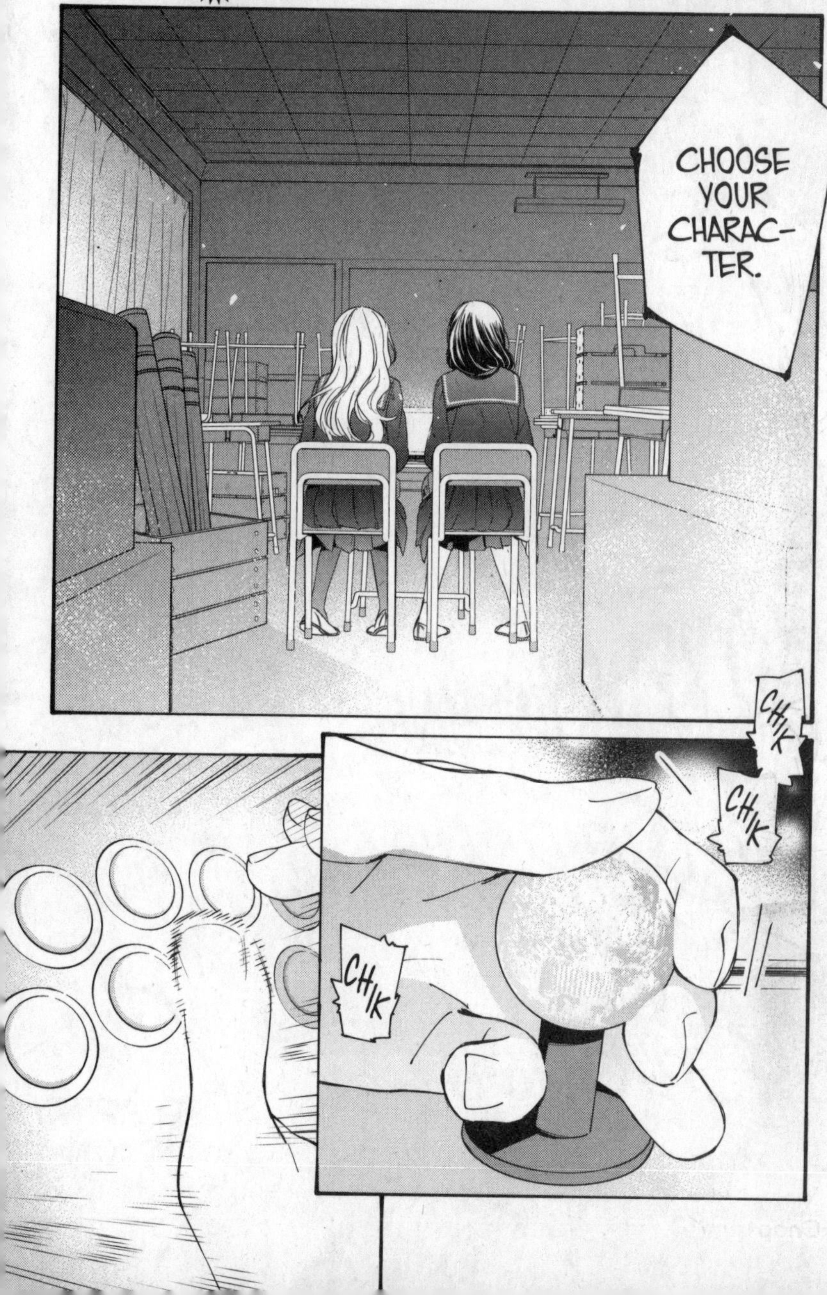
CHOOSE YOUR CHARAC-TER.
CHIK
CHIK
CHIK

BAM!!
HAGANE-SENPAI
HAGANE-SENPAI!
BAM!!
SECRETARY NEKOMI
SECRETARY NEKOMI!

WHEW...
PHEW...
AM I...
SERIOUSLY GOING THROUGH WITH THIS?!

ふっ…
HUFF...
……
ふっ…
HUFF...
ドキ
BA-DUMP
ドキ
BA-DUMP
はぁ
HAAH...
……
はっ…
HUFF...
HERE WE GO...

99
READY?
CHAOS
CHAOS
ZWSH
F-I-GHT
HELLO AGAIN...

TO THE FIGHTING GAMES I USED TO LOVE!!!
HUP!!
SPLATCH!
GYARGH!
2 HIT
3 HIT

SHA-PAH
BLOODY NAIL!!
6 HIT
JAB
5
4
ゴロッ
ROLL
SHWIP
ZWOOSH
KA-CHIK

SHAAANG
RISING FIIIST!
BLOCK
91
DASH
90
SPLORTCH
KO
2P WIN
BAM

......
......
UH......
G...
......!!
......
HOLY CRAP, SHE SUCKS!!
......
HEH...
HEH!
......
PFF, HEH... HAH!

......!
ふんしゅううううっ
HOOO...!!!!
BULGE
ピクッ
JOLT
Y...
Duh ...?
YEAH ...
FIRST TO THREE, RIGHT?!
......!
MITSUKI-SAN...

※Victory goes to the first player to score three wins. Common practice at fighting game tournaments.

...
......
UGH...
FIGHT!
99
Bloody Nail!!
TUP
GRAK
I GUESS I'M NOT SUR-PRISED.
THERE AREN'T MANY GIRLS OUT THERE WHO ARE INTO FIGHTING GAMES TO BEGIN WITH...
GRAK
GRAK
GRAK

92
HERE AT A PRESTIGIOUS ACADEMY FOR WELL-TO-DO YOUNG LADIES; NO LESS, ARE CLOSE TO...
THE ODDS OF CONVENIENTLY FINDING A DECENT PLAYER...
GRAK
GRAK
GRAK
BWSH
BAP
ZWOOP
THROW TECH
THAT'S FUNNY. NOW HER CHARACTER'S SUDDENLY ROCK-SOLID...
HUNH.
※Solid: Well-guarded with a solid defense.
※ Escaped the throw.
P

BA-GAAAM
HADOU SATSU!!!
COUNTER HIT
!!!
BA-SHIIING
ZWOOSH
HADOU SATSU!!!
HADOU SATSU!!!
HADOU SATSU!!!
HADOOOU !!!
......!!
AND NOW SHE'S SPAMMING ME WITH HADOUS!!
THWACK
IN THAT CASE...!
CHAOS

I'LL EXPEND MY CHAOS GAUGE ONCE IT'S FILLED...
AND USE AN EX CROUCHING NAIL TO SLIP THROUGH HER PROJECTILE AND BRING HER INTO CLOSE RANGE. THEN IT'S MY TURN TO GO ON THE OFFENSIVE!!
※EX Special Attacks
These super-powered special attacks can be unleashed by using the Chaos Gauge. These moves are stronger than normal special moves and sometimes come with special bonuses such as projectile invincibility.
CHAOS
I'LL SLIP PAST HER NEXT HADOU...!!
ボ
BOOMF
※Hadou feint.
BRING IT!!
FWIP

UR-RAGH!
THWAM
??!
HADOU!!
WHUMP
HADOU SATSU!!
WHUMP
WHA-WHUMP
HADOOOU !!!
NGH!
UGH...!
SKA-SKSHHH
HADOU SATSU!!!
......
TUMP
BOOSH
LET'S SEE HOW SHE LIKES THIS!!

DODGE
RISING...
ZWISH
56
FIIIIIIST!!!
SHA-BAAAAM
BAM
BAM
BAM
BAM
BAM
KO

WHA...?
THAT ROUND...
SHE SHRUGGED OFF MY ATTACKS WITH HER STRANGE, WALL-LIKE DEFENSE...
THEN BLASTED ME LIKE HER LIFE DEPENDED ON IT AS SOON AS I CAME TOO CLOSE!!
WHILE I FOCUSED ON HER PROJECTILE SPAM, WAITING FOR MY CHANCE TO BREAK THROUGH, SHE CHARGED ME WITH A FORWARD DASH INSTEAD.
FWIP
56
I TRIED TO FAKE HER OUT WITH A DECEPTIVE JUMP-IN AND HIT HER WITH A CROSS-UP AS A LAST-DITCH EFFORT...
BAM
BAM
BUT SHE WHIPPED AROUND AND NAILED ME WITH A FLAWLESS ANTI-AIR EX RISING FIST!!
BAM
......

※Cross-up: a jumping attack executed while soaring over the opponent's head. This attack is meant to reverse the players' positions, forcing the defensive player to reverse their input directions.

FOR SOME REASON...
I ALMOST FEEL LIKE I COULD CRY.
PA-SHING
PLAYER 1
Rematch
Return to character select.
PLAYER 2
Rematch
Return to ch
......
......
......
......?
HEY!
UM, MITSUKI-SAN? YOU HAVE TO PRESS REMATCH ...
UH...

……
THAT WAS... HONESTLY GORGEOUS.
I'LL ADMIT IT.
かぁ BLUSH..
THAT LAST FIGHT, AND...
AND YOU TOO, SHIRAYURI-SAMA!
THE EXACT OPPOSITE OF THE GIRL I AM NOW. THE ONE WHO TOSSED HER GAMES ASIDE...
DESPERATE TO BE A "PROPER YOUNG LADY."
WHAT MAKES YOU SHINE LIKE THAT...?

THAT'S...

SOMEONE'S COMING.
HUH?!
CLOMP...
CRAP!
CLOMP...
BWISH
LET'S HIDE!
TH-THERE'S NOWHERE *TO* HIDE IN HERE!
CLUNK
CRAAAASH
!

HEY!!
WHAT IN TARNATION DIDJA DO THAT FER?!
※Why'd you do that?
D-DON'T LOOK AT ME!
TH-THE CHAIR WAS STACKED IN A PRECARIOUS POSITION! I BARELY NUDGED IT!
IS SOME-ONE IN THERE?
EEP!
......
"DIDN'T YOU KNOW, AYA-SAN? GAMES ARE PROHIBITED IN KUROMI'S DORMS."
"WHY, SOME STUDENTS EVEN GOT EXPELLED FOR BRINGING CONSOLES ONTO CAMPUS!"
EXPELLED
MUST HAVE COME FROM IN HERE...
SLIDE

KRAK
KRIIIISH

SKRRRSH
WHA...
WHAT THE HECK?!

…
IS YOUR LAPTOP OKAY?
And your arcade stick?
ハァ…
HUFF…
YES.
I THINK SO…
ゼェ…
WHEEZE…

YOINK
GOOD.
THEN THIS IS WHERE WE SPLIT UP.
MITSUKI-SAN.
I'LL SEE YOU TOMORROW.

CHAK
BUT I SHOWED UP THE NEXT DAY...
ONLY TO FIND OUR SECRET CLASS-ROOM LOCKED UP TIGHT.
AND THEN...
ATTENTION, ALL FIRST-YEARS.
THERE WILL BE AN ASSEMBLY SHORTLY.
AFTER EVENING ROLL CALL, PLEASE MAKE HASTE TO THE ASSEMBLY ROOM LOCATED ON THE SECOND FLOOR OF BUILDING A.

ASSEMBLY ROOM
GOOD EVENING, LADIES.
TO THOSE OF YOU WHO MAY NOT KNOW ME, I AM FUJIMIYA MORINO, PRESIDENT OF THE DORMITORY AFFAIRS COMMITTEE.
ALLOW ME TO EXPLAIN WHY YOU ARE ALL GATHERED HERE TONIGHT.
AFTER SCHOOL YESTER-DAY...
A CERTAIN INDIVIDUAL SMASHED ONE OF THE WINDOWS IN A CLASSROOM LOCATED ON THE GROUND FLOOR OF THE SPECIAL CLASSROOM ANNEX.
MURMUR...
ざわ・・

……
FORTUNATELY, A JANITOR WAS CLOSE ENOUGH TO WITNESS THE EVENT.
UNFORTUNATELY, IT ALL HAPPENED TOO QUICKLY FOR HIM TO SEE THAT PERSON'S FACE. HOWEVER...
HE WAS ABLE TO COLLECT AN ARTICLE WE BELIEVE BELONGS TO ONE OF THE PERPETRATORS.
TO WIT...
A RED RIBBON BELONGING TO A FIRST-YEAR STUDENT.
"SEE YOU TOMORROW."
THAT ABSOLUTE FRICKIN' IDIOT!!
What a rookie mistake!!
WHICH BRINGS ME TO MY POINT.

DO ANY OF YOU KNOW TO WHOM THIS RIBBON MIGHT BELONG?
HUSH...
SMILE
VERY WELL.
MURMUR...
"THEN WE SHALL SAY THE COLLECTIVE RESPONSIBILITY RESTS ON THE SHOULDERS OF ALL FIRST-YEARS."
"FOR THE NEXT MONTH, YOU WILL ALL CLEAN THE DORMITORY FROM TOP TO BOTTOM BEFORE MORNING ROLL CALL."
MURMUR...
MURMUR...
GOSH, SOMEONE BROKE A WINDOW...
I HAD NO IDEA WE HAD SUCH *BARBARIANS* HERE AT KUROMI GIRLS'.
HOW DREADFUL... STARTING TOMORROW, WE'LL HAVE TO WAKE UP A FULL HOUR EARLIER EVERY DAY.
......

407
"SLOW YOUR ROLL."
THAT SOME HIGHER GODLIKE BEING...
SEEMS TO BE SENDING ME RIGHT NOW.
THAT'S THE MESSAGE...

I'VE ALREADY INCONVE-NIENCED THE OTHER FIRST-YEARS.
RIGHT NOW, I'M ONE WRONG MOVE FROM GETTING EXPELLED.
I GAVE IN AND PLAYED A GAME YESTERDAY, SURE.
BUT REALLY, THE RISK/REWARD WASN'T WORTH IT.
SPIN
TWIRL
RIGHT.
FLIP
NOTHING PERSONAL, SHIRAYURI-SAMA.
DO THE SMART THING, AYA.
GAMING IS THE LAST THING YOU NEED TO DO RIGHT NOW.
SNATCH
......
BUT...

WOW! YOU'RE A PEN-TWIRLING WHIZ!
HI-GEEE!!!
"HIGGY"?
NATSUME-SAN! GIVE ME SOME WARNING BEFORE YOU HIT ME WITH A GAP-CLOSER!!
I almost started thinking out loud!!
BA-DUMP
BA-DUMP
I'M SORRY, A WHAT?
ANY-WAY...
WHAT CAN I HELP YOU WITH TODAY?
OH! PHYSICS, IF YOU DON'T MIND.
IT'S JUST...
I DON'T KNOW.
I CAN'T SEEM TO THINK ABOUT ANYTHING ELSE...

THANK YOU EVER SO MUCH AS ALWAYS, AYA-SAN!
YOU'RE ALWAYS WILLING TO HELP ME WHENEVER I NEED IT. I DON'T KNOW WHAT I'D DO WITHOUT YOU!!
YOU'RE SO GOOD AT OUR COURSE-WORK.
I'VE BEEN MEANING TO ASK. DO YOU LOVE LEARNING THAT MUCH?
I WOULDN'T GO *THAT* FAR.
BLUSH
BUT I DON'T MIND IT.
I JUST GRIND IT OUT LIKE MY LIFE DEPENDS ON IT. KIND OF LIKE A PUZZLE...
YOUR LIFE??
WAIT... HUH?
LOVE...
LOVE?

※Like your life depends on it: when an opponent uses the same actions again and again, they are said to be "***ing like their life depends on it." In practice, it often means a brief period of time.

"HOW DO YOU SHINE LIKE THAT?"
WELL...
I'M...
NOT QUITE SURE. BUT...
......
WHEN YOU GIVE YOUR ALL TO SOMETHING YOU LOVE...
THEN YOU'LL NATURALLY SHINE ALL ON YOUR OWN. RIGHT?

ATTENTION ALL STUDENTS.
QUIET TIME IS NOW OVER.

PLEASE BEGIN PREPARING FOR BED.
ONCE AGAIN...
ALL OF THOSE EMOTIONS LOCKED AWAY BY THE IMPACT OF CRASHING THROUGH THE WINDOW...
HAVE RETURNED IN FULL FORCE!!

AYA WAS PLAGUED BY ONE PERSISTENT THOUGHT: WOULD ANYTHING EVER GRAB HER THE WAY FIGHTING GAMES DID IN HER CHILDHOOD?
SHUFF...
FEAR...
ANXIETY...
AND WORRY COMPELLED HER TO CHOOSE THE PATH THAT WOULD TAKE HER FURTHEST AWAY FROM FIGHTING GAMES.
SHUFF...
"WHEN YOU GIVE YOUR ALL TO SOME-THING YOU LOVE..."
IT WAS A SHALLOW COMMENT SHE WOULD HAVE EASILY LAUGHED OFF AT ANY OTHER TIME.
BUT ONLY IF...
THOSE WORDS HADN'T COME FROM A WOMAN UNDENIABLY BLESSED WITH GOOD LOOKS...
A REGAL BEAR-ING...
AND A PURE, UNAFFECTED PASSION FOR VIDEO GAMES!
SHUFF...

IF ONLY IT HADN'T COME FROM SHIRAYURI-SAMA!!!

I'M DONE.
I'LL QUIT FIGHTING GAMES FOREVER.
BUT BEFORE I DO...

INTO THE HEAT OF BATTLE...!
GO FOR IT!
I'M GOING TO SHAT-TER HER HEART...
INTO TEENY-TINY PIECES!!
Chapter 2 /END

Chapter 3 That's Why I Deny You

......
"AYA-SAN? WHAT IS THIS ALL ABOUT?"

YOU RACED OUT OF THE ROOM LOOKING AS ANGRY AS A DEMON...
AND NOW YOU'VE RETURNED WITH SHIRAYURI-SAMA OF ALL PEOPLE?
CLAP
WHY, I HAD NO IDEA YOU WERE ACQUAIN-TANCES!
She's gorgeous even up close...
NATSUME-SAN...
PLEASE DON'T PRESS ME FOR DETAILS...
BUT CAN YOU DO ME A *HUGE* FAVOR AND STAY IN SHIRAYURI-SAMA'S ROOM JUST FOR TONIGHT?

......!!!
I...
SUPPOSE I DON'T MIND, BUT...
BUT DOES THAT MEAN...
ERM...
CLNK
WHAT?
I MERELY WONDER IF...
ドキ
BA-DUMP
AH-HEM...
ドキ
BA-DUMP
TH-THAT IS TO SAY...!!
OH, YOU KNOW!
ドキ
BA-DMP
COULD YOU TWO POSSIBLY BE...UM...!!
CLENCH

THWONK
NO!! LOVE COMES IN MANY DIFFERENT FORMS!!
?!!
......
AYA-SAN...
STAGGER...
"I'M BEHIND YOU ONE HUNDRED PERCENT!!!"
CLENCH
SOMETHING TELLS ME WE'RE NOT ON THE SAME PAGE...
BUT AT LEAST SHE'S WILLING TO COOPERATE. THAT'S ALL THAT MATTERS FOR NOW!
......
IRON SEMPAI 4
LOADING..
FIVE.

THE FIRST TO FIVE WINS.
IS THAT FINE BY YOU?
......
I KNOW...
I'M ONLY PROJECTING MY SELF-LOATHING ONTO HER.
YEAH...
LET'S GO WITH THAT.

99
READY?
BUT SHE'S STILL GOING DOWN.
CHAOS
CHAOS
FIGHT

98
FIRST AND FOREMOST, I'M GONNA CRUSH HER!!
BOOSH
BA-
CHAOS
CHAOS
GA-
TAK
BAM
TAKKA

WHAM
AS SOON AS THE FIGHT BEGAN, WE CHARGED AT EACH OTHER WITH THREE PERFECTLY SIMULTANEOUS TRADES.
LIKE A REFLECTION OF OUR UNWILLING-NESS TO WAIT ANOTHER SECOND!!

WHA-
PISH
HADOU!!!
2 HIT
DUCK
!
THE SECOND SHE SEES MY GAUGE FILL...
THERE IT IS.
CHAOS
SHE'LL BLUFF WITH A QUICK CROUCH, AS IF SHE'S ABOUT TO UNLEASH A HADOU SATSU IN MY DIRECTION.
THEN SHE'LL BAIT ME WITH A CROUCH AND A MID-PUNCH--THE SAME MOTIONS NEEDED TO TRIGGER A HADOU SATSU.
SWIP
SWIP
BOOF

※ The command string for Hadou Satsu is ↓ ↘→P. Because of this, the player will always crouch just before it is triggered.

BUT SHE WON'T GET ME THIS TIME.
......
I'LL PRETEND I'M WAITING FOR HER HADOU, AND THEN...
SWOOSH
PA-KRAAAK
!!!
I'LL COUNTER HER FORWARD DASH WITH A LIGHT PUNCH...

THWACK
SKRSH
BWAK
4 HIT
GORE STING-ER!!!
※Corner: the far edge of the stage, where the screen can scroll no further.
AND SEND HER FLYING INTO THE CORNER WHILE INFLICTING MAXIMUM DAMAGE!
THONK
CHAOS
CHAOS
I CAN'T STAND BEING INDECISIVE.

I ALWAYS KNEW...
THAT GETTING INTO KUROMI GIRLS' ACADEMY...
AND BECOMING A PROPER YOUNG LADY...
DIDN'T GUARANTEE I'D FIND ANYTHING THAT WOULD CAPTIVATE ME THE WAY FIGHTING GAMES DID WHEN I WAS A KID.
ZWOOSH
THE ONLY CERTAINTY IN THIS SITUATION...
IS THAT I WON'T FIND ANYTHING UNLESS I KEEP PRESSING FORWARD.
BUT I WON'T MAKE NEARLY AS MUCH PROGRESS DOWN THIS ROAD...
IF I MOVE FORWARD WHILE DOUBTING MYSELF.
"YOU'LL NATURALLY SHINE ALL ON YOUR OWN."

THAT IS WHY I DENY YOU!!!
IF I WANT TO CHARGE FULL-SPEED INTO TOMORROW AND ALL THE DAYS AHEAD...
HESITATION IS NOT AN OPTION.
KA-KLUNK

THEN FOR MY OWN FUTURE!!!
I WILL DENY YOU, SHIRAYURI!!!

THIS IS SECRETARY NEKOMI'S WINNING GAMEPLAN!!!
WHOOSH
AN ALL-OUT SLAUGHTER AT THE EDGE OF THE STAGE...RIGHT WHERE THERE'S NO AVENUE OF ESCAPE!!
POW
THIS IS WHERE IT ENDS!!
WHAK
DIE, SHIRA-YURI!!!

GRAB
SHWIP
FWOOSH
PA-SHING
THROW TECH
SWFF...
GRAB
PA-SHING
THROW TECH

TMP
BOOSH
BLOODY NAIL!!!
PWIK
SWF
SWF
......
JAB
SWOOP

SPINNING HURRICANE ELBOW!!!
BAM
!!
ZWAP
ZWAP
2 HIT
3 HIT
WHUD
SKSH
......!!!
SHE BROKE OUT OF THE CORNER...
AND BRUSHED OFF MY ATTACK!!
TUP

SHA-
BOOOOM
AAAAAHH!!
BAM
BAM
BAM
BAAM
K.O.

......
HUH ...?
WAIT...
WHAT?
WHAT THE HECK WAS THAT? SHE WAS INVINCIBLE!
INVINCIBLE MOVES!!
AFTER TRIGGERING CERTAIN SPECIAL ATTACKS, THE PLAYER IS *INVINCIBLE* FOR A CERTAIN NUMBER OF FRAMES.
EX Gore Stinger Total invincibilit for 1-10 frames
EX Rising Fis Total invincibili for 1-15 frames
IF YOU'RE ENJOYING THE EFFECT OF I-FRAMES, ENEMY ATTACKS OR THROWS THAT WOULD NORMALLY LEAVE YOU BEGGING FOR MERCY...

ARE COMPLETELY IGNORED, GIVING YOU AN OPENING TO BEAT YOUR HELPLESS OPPONENT TO A PULP!!
THIS IS THE POWER OF AN INVINCIBILE MOVE!!!
BUT IF THE OPPONENT GUARDS SUCH AN ATTACK, YOU'RE LEFT WITH A GAPING HOLE IN YOUR DEFENSE!
IN OTHER WORDS, IT'S A DOUBLE-EDGED SWORD THAT OPENS YOU UP TO BRUTAL AMOUNTS OF DAMAGE!!!
NRGH...
AAAARGH!!!
NOW I'M PISSED!!
GRT
CREEEEAK

SHE LAUNCHED AN UNSAFE INVINCIBLE MOVE FROM THE CORNER OF THE SCREEN...
JUST TO DENY MY ALL-OUT ATTACK?!
NO... THAT'S NOT IT!
BA-DUMP
SHE BROKE THROUGH THAT CORNER-PRESSURE NO-MAN'S-LAND WITH HER IRON DEFENSE...
BA-DUMP
ONLY TO BLAST ME WITH A WAKE-UP SHE DIDN'T EVEN NEED TO USE!!
FWOO...
※Unsafe attack: As the name implies, the player uses a special move that they acknowledge may be risky, but throw caution to the wind and do it anyway.
NRGH... I'LL KILL HER!
GRIKK...
NO, NO, SLOW DOWN. DEEP BREATHS.
GRIT
LOSE YOUR COOL AND YOU LOSE THE GAME.
THAT'S FIGHTING GAMES 101!!
HOWEVER.

IN THE SECOND SET...
SHIRAYURI-SAMA MADE A CRITICAL MISTAKE. THIS OPENED HER UP TO A RAPID BARRAGE OF WAKE-UP ATTACKS FROM AYA, RESULTING IN HER VICTORY.
AFTER THAT, AYA CLOSED THE DISTANCE BETWEEN THE TWO. HER VICTORY SEEMED ALL BUT ASSURED...
ONLY FOR SHIRAYURI-SAMA TO SLIP THROUGH AYA'S ONSLAUGHT, GOING ON TO STEAL THE SET.
NRGH...IT'S CRAZY HOW SHE CAN OVERCOME JUST ABOUT ANYTHING!
FOR BETTER OR WORSE...
THAT'S WHAT MAKES HER HAGANE-SENPAI SO SCARY.
BUT SHE PUTS MORE STOCK INTO HER RESILIENCE THAN SHE SHOULD, AND COMMITS TO ALL KINDS OF GARBAGE SUICIDE MOVES.

PWOK
WHY ARE YOU SO DESPERATE TO WIN?
OUR STAKES ARE COMPLETELY DIFFERENT HERE.
YOUR FUTURE ISN'T RIDING ON THIS FIGHT THE WAY MINE IS.
THOOM
KO
NOW THE SET COUNT...
IS FOUR TO FOUR!!!
※Since they are playing a first to five match, the next set will decide the winner.

SHUFF...
SHUFF...
WHAP
YANK
FWUP
......

SHUFF...

SHUFF...
ドクン!!
BA-DUMP!!
Chapter 8 /END

ドクン…
BA-DUMP…
Chapter 4
ドクンッ…!!
BA-DUMP…!!
OH…
BALLS.

SHE JUST WON'T STOP PLAYING MIND GAMES WITH ME!!
ドキン!!
BA-DUMP!!
ドキン!!
BA-DUMP!!
ドキン!!
BA-DUMP!!
GOD, HER EYELASHES ARE LONG...
Chapter 4 G.G.W.P.

......
JUST WHEN IT LOOKS LIKE SHE COMMANDS THE PLAYING FIELD WITH WATER-LIKE STILLNESS...
SHE'LL COME AT ME WITH AN INSANE FORWARD DASH...
STRAINING TO PUSH HERSELF FOR NO DISCERNABLE REASON.
YOU P...
HAHEE!
P-PLAY...
FUH...!
FIGHT-ING...!!
PANT!
Y-Y-YOU T-T-TOTALLY PLAY FIGHTING GAMES, DON'T YOU?!
SPLAP
※Forward dash: A move used to close the gap between opponents in one smooth motion. Conversely, it can also mean taking a risk to perform a move.
I JUST DON'T GET IT.
I DON'T GET HER...AND I DON'T GET THE WAY SHE PLAYS HAGANE-SENPAI, EITHER.
HER WEIRD RESILIENCE.
HER SLIPPERI-NESS.
I SHOULD HAVE BEEN ABLE TO BREAK HER IN TWO WITH A PERFECT 5-0 SWEEP...

WE'RE DOWN TO OUR LAST SET...
BUT VICTORY ISN'T ENOUGH FOR ME.
SHUFF...
SINCE OUR BATTLE IS SO CLOSE...
EVEN IF I'M LUCKY ENOUGH TO PUMMEL HER INTO SUBMISSION, IF I DON'T UNDERSTAND THE LOGIC BEHIND HER GAME...
I'LL NEVER BE ABLE TO MAKE HER FEEL HER DEFEAT!!
THE KEY TO MAKING HER FEEL LIKE SHE'S LOST IS...
OH!
MITSUKI-SAN...
YOUR HEART.

THUMP...
IT'S...
THUMP...
BEATING TERRIBLY FAST.
SLIDE...
THUMP
THUMP

DO YOU ADMIT DEFEAT?
HUH?

YOU'RE AFRAID TO CONTINUE OUR MATCH, AREN'T YOU? BECAUSE OF THE FOOTSTEPS WE JUST HEARD.
I REALLY DON'T MIND.
WE CAN JUST SAY I'VE WON.
CREAK
UH, NO?
I'M STILL GOING TO PLAY.
We've already made it to the last set.

......
HMPH.
THIS...
......
THIS LITTLE PUNK!

TAK
PWOK
DUNNN
PLAYER 2
Rematch
Return to character select.
99
READY...
CHAOS

FIGHT!
HEH...
TAK
TAK
CHAK
CHAK
HEH HEH!
NO, I THINK I UNDERSTAND NOW.
KTAK

SHE'S JUST A BIG, GIANT BABY!
"SHUT UP AND FIGHT ME!!"
THAT'S WHY SHE CRIES WHEN THINGS DON'T GO HER WAY...
SWOOP
TAK
BLOODY NAIL!!!

SHE DOESN'T THINK ABOUT TOMOR-ROW.
RISING FIST!!!
WHA-BAAAAM
HER VICTORY. THIS MOMENT. THAT'S ALL SHE CARES ABOUT.

OH...
THAT'S HOW IT WAS.
BACK WHEN I WAS A KID.
I NEVER THOUGHT ABOUT TOMORROW.
I NEVER THOUGHT ABOUT ANYTHING.
WHAM
SKSH

GORE STING-ER!!!
3 HIT
BAM
BAM
BAM
I GAVE IT EVERY-THING I HAD, WITHOUT ANY RHYME OR REASON.
IRK
HA HA!
NRGH!!

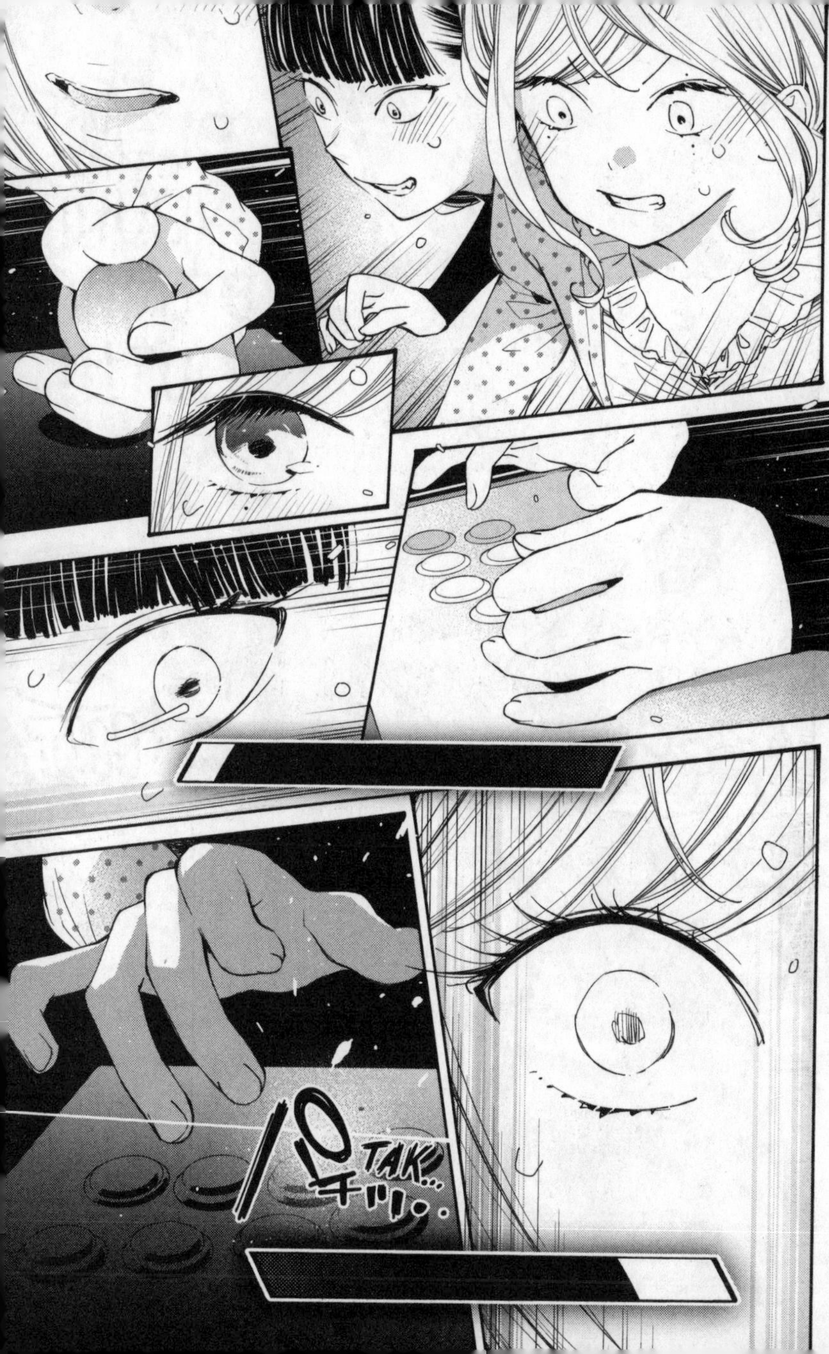
TAK...

I'LL BLOW YOUR BRAINS OUT!!!
I'LL SLICE YOU TO RIBBONS!!!

VRMM
GRIK
GRIK

SPLURRRTCH
Fatality
......!

AWWW YEAH!!!

はっ
GASP!
AH...
......!!!

......
THANK YOU...
FOR A GAME WELL PLAYED...
カッ
KLAT
カン
TNK
カン
TNK
カン
TNK

ばさっ FWUMP
……
……
KUROMI GIRLS' ACAD

!
SWISH...
UH...
HEY, UH...
ABOUT YESTER-DAY...
......
TMP...
TMP...

The next day.
ボ HONNNNG...
ボ HONG...
ボ HONNNNG...
......
DIDJA HEAR? THE SEQUEL TO π2 IS OUT!!
LET'S HAVE ANOTHER TOURNEY AT TAKEDA'S PLACE!!
I DUNNO, WE'VE ALL BEEN TOO BUSY WITH CLUBS AND STUFF TO PRACTICE.
'SIDES...

TAKEDA SOLD HIS ARCADE STICKS AND HIS SYSTEM ANYWAY.
Said he needed to buy some kendo gear.
OH...
GAMES ARE GREAT 'N ALL...
BUT LET'S HAVE A SOCCER MATCH SOMETIME, MITSUKI!!
Later!!
HUH??
TMP TMP TMP...
SERI-OUSLY?
SOCCER?
"I'M TOTALLY GONNA MAKE YOU CRY THIS TIME!!"
......
......
FILTHY LIARS...
......

YOU CAN'T PLAY...
IF YOU'RE ALL ALONE, YOU KNOW...
......
SHOULD I APOLOGIZE?
WHAT AM I SUP-POSED TO SAY?
"SORRY FOR KICKING YOUR ASS"?
THAT'D ONLY COME OFF AS BAD SPORTS-MANSHIP...
はーーー
SIGH...
ゴソ
SHUFF
ゴソ
SHUFF

WHOA!! WHERE'D YOU COME FROM?!
ビクゥ JOLT
EEP!!
DON'T SCREAM LIKE THAT OUT OF NOWHERE!!
I ONLY SCREAMED BECAUSE YOU SHOWED UP OUT OF NOWHERE!!
WHAT ARE YOU EVEN DOING HERE?!
THAT'S OBVIOUS, ISN'T IT?
ゴッ TNK
CLEARLY.
I CAME TO FIGHT YOU.
!
......
WHAT IS UP WITH THIS GIRL?

1P
LOSE
1
Wins
2P
WIN
5
Wins
Results
Rematch
Return to character select
Results
Rematch
Return to character select
I won't be the student council's dog, got it? Now run on back to your masters.

......
SERI-OUSLY?
WHEN DID YOU HOP INTO TRAINING MODE?
HUH?
HER GAME STYLE DID A 180 FROM BEFORE...SHE TURTLED LIKE CRAZY! I COULDN'T BREAK THROUGH HER DEFENSE AT ALL!!
AND THAT'S NOT ALL.
SHE'S RESPONDING TO MY ATTACKS WITH WAY MORE ACCURACY NOW, TOO!!
LOSE
I MEAN, THE OLD CLASS-ROOM'S LOCKED UP, RIGHT?
SO I DOUBT YOU COULD FIND A TIME OR A PLACE TO WHALE ON A TRAINING DUMMY.

※Training mode: An area where one practices moves. Synonymous with gaining skill.

I USED MY MENTAL TRAINING DUMMY.
YOUR WUH?
I PRACTICED IN MY HEAD.
I WAS BORED IN CLASS, ANYWAY.
I DID IT ALL DAY YESTERDAY.
......
KSH
MMM...!

GG, WP!

"I'M TOTALLY GONNA MAKE YOU CRY THIS TIME!!"
HA HA!

NEXT TIME, YOU'RE DEAD MEAT!!
~Young Ladies Don't Play Fighting Games~ 1 /END